A MINDBOGGLING HISTORY OF SCIENTISTS AND INVENTORS

Izzi Howell

FRANKLIN WATTS
LONDON•SYDNEY

Franklin Watts
First published in Great Britain in 2016 by The Watts Publishing Group

Produced for Franklin Watts by
White-Thomson Publishing Ltd
www.wtpub.co.uk

Credits
Series Editor: Izzi Howell
Series Designer: Rocket Design (East Anglia) Ltd
Series Consultant: Philip Parker

The publisher would like to thank the following for permission to reproduce their pictures: Alamy/Classic Image 7; Alamy/Stephen Sykes 20; Alamy/David A. Barnes 22; Alamy/Pictorial Press 23 (bottom); Bridgeman Ms Ar 5847 fol.5, Abu Zayd in the library at Basra, from 'The Maqamat' (The Meetings) by Al-Hariri, c.1240 (gouache on paper), Al-Wasiti, Yahya ibn Mahmud (13th Century) / Bibliotheque Nationale, Paris, France / Archives Charmet; Dreamstime/Claudiodivizia 15 (bottom right); Mary Evans Picture Library 9 (left); i-Stock/GeorgiosArt cover (top right); i-Stock/BasieB 9 (bottom right); Mary Evans Picture Library/Fonollosa/Iberfoto 11 (top); Mary Evans Picture Library/Iberfoto 22 (right); Mary Evans Picture Library/Natural History Museum 23 (top); Mary Evans Picture Library/SZ Photo/Scheri 25 (top); NASA/ NASA, ESA, and M. Livio and the Hubble 20th Anniversary Team (STScI) 26; NASA 27 (top right); NASA/JPL-CaltechMSSS 28-29; SPL/SHEILA TERRY/SCIENCE PHOTO LIBRARY 18; Shutterstock/Deyan Georgiev cover (bottom right); Shutterstock/samantha grandy 4-5; Shutterstock/Morphart Creation 8; Shutterstock/Nikita Maykov 13 (bottom); Shutterstock/HildaWeges Photography 15 (top); Shutterstock/lolloj 15 (bottom right); Shutterstock/Tomasz Bidermann 16; Shutterstock/Everett Historical 25 (bottom left); Shutterstock/Dragon images 27 (centre); Shutterstock/drserg 27 (bottom right); Shutterstock/AuntSpray 28; Stefan Chabluk 31; Wellcome Library, London 14; Wellcome Library 17 (left); Wellcome Library, London 19; Wellcome Library, London 21; Wellcome Library, London 24; Werner Forman Archive/Spink and Son Ltd 13 (top); Wikimedia/International Dunhang Project 10; Wikimedia/Zeng Gongliang, Ding Du, and Yang Weide. All design elements from Shutterstock.

ISBN 978 1 4451 4937 0

Printed in China

Franklin Watts
An imprint of
Hachette Children's Group
Part of The Watts Publishing Group
Carmelite House
50 Victoria Embankment
London EC4Y 0DZ

An Hachette UK Company
www.hachette.co.uk

www.franklinwatts.co.uk

Words in **bold** appear in the glossary on pages 30 and 31.

CONTENTS

SCIENTISTS AND INVENTORS THROUGH HISTORY

Over time, many scientists have pondered big questions about science and the natural world. Through dangerous experiments and tricky tests, they learned how to look for answers and prove that they were correct. Little by little, scientists have come to understand many of the mysteries of our planet.

With the help of incredible inventors, we have learned how to use science to our advantage. Brilliant but wacky machines from the past have inspired the inventions that we use every day. Read on to find out about some of the greatest scientists and inventors of all time and how their discoveries and creations changed our world forever.

This timeline shows you the names, nationalities and dates of the people mentioned in this book.

Thales of Miletus (Greece) 620–546 BCE

Hippocrates (Greece) 460–375

NORTH AMERICA

ATLANTIC OCEAN

SOUTH AMERICA

Patented over 1,000 inventions

Built and flew the world's first successful aeroplane

Nikola Tesla (Serbia/USA) 1856–1943

Pierre Curie (France) 1859–1906

Marie Curie (Poland/France) 1867–1934

Wright brothers (USA) 1867–1912 and 1871–1948

Albert Einstein (Germany/USA) 1879–1955

Margaret Hamilton (USA) 1936–

Stephen Hawking (England) 1942–

Tim Berners-Lee (England) 1955–

Mark Zuckerberg (USA) 1984–

Plato (Greece) 428–347
Aristotle (Greece) 384–322
Archimedes (Greece) c.287–212
Cai Lun (China) CE c.62–121
Ptolemy (Greece/Egypt) c.100–170
Avicenna (Uzbekistan/Iran) 980–1037
Leonardo da Vinci (Italy) 1452–1519
Nicolaus Copernicus (Poland) 1473–1543
Tycho Brahe (Denmark) 1546–1601
Galileo Galilei (Italy) 1564–1642
Johannes Kepler (Germany) 1571–1630
William Harvey (England) 1578–1657
Robert Hooke (England) 1635–1703
Isaac Newton (England) 1643–1727
James Watt (Scotland) 1736–1819
Edward Jenner (England) 1749–1823
Charles Babbage (England) 1791–1871
Charles Darwin (England) 1809–1882
Ada Lovelace (England) 1815–1852
Louis Pasteur (France) 1822–1895
Thomas Edison (USA) 1847–1931
Convinced scientists that they needed to make observations to prove their theories
Came up with the perfect recipe for paper
Built his own telescope and used it to prove that the Earth moves around the Sun
Collected spit from the mouth of a rabid dog to use in his rabies vaccine
EUROPE
ASIA
AFRICA
PACIFIC OCEAN
AUSTRALASIA
ANTARCTICA

GIFTED GREEKS

For thousands of years, ancient people used religion to explain the natural world until some brainy ancient **Greek philosophers** started looking for more scientific answers.

Explaining earthquakes

In the 6th century BCE, philosophers in the city of Athens, Greece, started to come up with some (fairly!) reasonable ideas about science, using nature rather than the **supernatural** as an explanation. The philosopher Thales of Miletus used his **theory** that the Earth floated on water in the sky to explain how earthquakes were caused – waves in the water, obviously!

SUPER SCIENTISTS

NAME: Hippocrates (460–375 BCE)

NATIONALITY: Greek

AKA: Illness investigator

ACHIEVEMENTS: Instead of praying to the gods for a cure, Hippocrates was one of the first **physicians** to look for natural reasons why his patients might be puking all over the place. Unfortunately, he was basically clueless about how the human body worked, as it was **taboo** to **dissect** humans in ancient Greece!

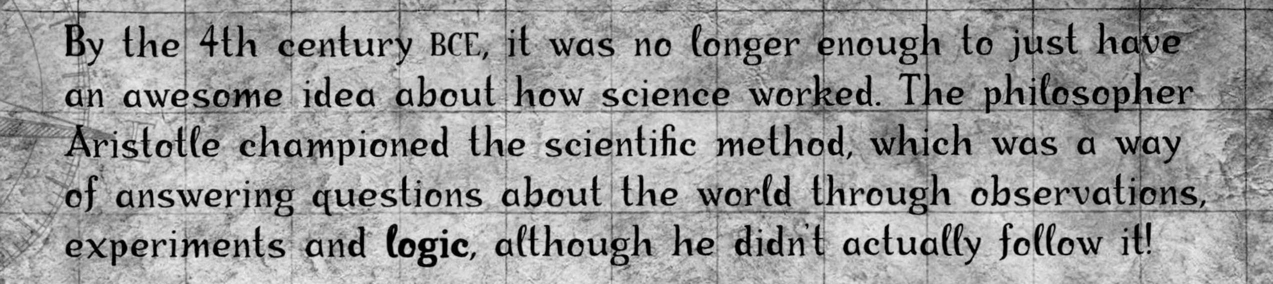

By the 4th century BCE, it was no longer enough to just have an awesome idea about how science worked. The philosopher Aristotle championed the scientific method, which was a way of answering questions about the world through observations, experiments and **logic**, although he didn't actually follow it!

HAVE YOU GOT WHAT IT TAKES?

PLATO'S PUPIL

TOP SKILL: A* in arguing

Many top Greek thinkers, including Aristotle, studied at the exclusive Academy in Athens. Their teacher was Plato, a seriously smart philosopher, who thought that the best way to learn how to be logical was to discuss problems out loud from different points of view. By squabbling with their classmates, his students learned how to defend their own theories and criticise others, which helped their theories become better.

Mainly male students attended Plato's Academy in Athens. Only two women were ever allowed to study there.

Now, where did I put my shirt?

EXPANDING EMPIRES

The Greek world grew larger in the late 4th century BCE, when Alexander the Great took over Egypt and parts of the Middle East. Cities such as Alexandria, Egypt, became a melting pot of people with fresh, exciting ideas about science.

Paying for papyrus

Science and learning in Alexandria flourished thanks to the ruling royal family. They spent a fortune building the largest library of the ancient world, filled with scientific texts written on **papyrus** scrolls. Sadly, the Library of Alexandria burned down in the 3rd century CE and the knowledge on the scrolls was lost forever.

INGENIOUS INVENTORS

NAME: Archimedes (287–212 BCE)

NATIONALITY: Greek

AKA: Lever lover

ACHIEVEMENTS: Archimedes was a superstar scientist who studied in Alexandria. By applying maths and logic to practical problems, he came up with useful inventions that lifted heavy objects and took water from rivers. He's best known for experimenting in the bathtub about how water moves around objects and for shouting *'Eureka!'* ('I've found it' in Greek) when he finally found the answer!

HE SAID WHAT?

'Give me a lever and a place to stand and I will move the world.'

Archimedes

Greek scientists, such as Ptolemy, carried on studying and writing about science in Greek, even after Greece became part of the **Roman Empire** in 146 BCE. Ptolemy came up with the idea that the Earth was at the centre of the universe, a theory believed to be true up until the **Middle Ages**. The Romans were more interested in engineering and the key to their magnificent buildings, bridges and **aqueducts** was concrete.

HAVE YOU GOT WHAT IT TAKES?

CONCRETE CHEMIST

MUST HAVE: Access to a volcano

Early concrete recipes included horsehair and volcanic ash, but the best Roman concrete was strengthened by the volcanic rock pumice (used today to scrape dead skin off your feet). It could even set underwater, which was useful for building bridges. By combining brick and stone with concrete, the Romans could build large curved arches and domes to support the weight of their huge structures.

This concrete and stone Roman aqueduct still stands today near the city of Nîmes in southern France.

DYNASTIES AND DISCOVERIES

Chinese inventors have come up with some of the world's finest inventions, from everyday favourites such as wheelbarrows to world-changing technology, such as paper, gunpowder, printing and the compass.

Taking notes

Before the invention of paper, information was recorded on papyrus or fabric, which were fragile and expensive. Only the most important ideas could be written down. After paper was invented in China in the 2nd century CE, it spread to the rest of the world via **Silk Road** travellers who traded with India and the Islamic world. Paper was cheap, durable and easy to make, meaning that written information could be easily shared across continents and over centuries.

NAME: Cai Lun (CE 50–121)

NATIONALITY: Chinese

AKA: Paper pioneer

ACHIEVEMENTS: When not working at the emperor's palace, Cai Lun worked on his pet project – paper. The winning method was boiling a bizarre brew of rags, fishing nets, tree bark and hemp, and then collecting and drying the fibres on a smooth mat to make paper.

The oldest printed book, the Diamond Sutra, was made in China in CE 868, 500 years before printing kicked off in Europe (see page 16).

MUST BE ABLE TO:

find an upgrade

The first compasses from the Han Dynasty (206 BCE to CE 220) were spoon-shaped and used for fortune telling. In the Tang Dynasty (CE 618 to 907) inventors upgraded the spoon to a thin needle, which accurately pointed north. By the Song Dynasty (CE 960 to 1279), brainy sailors had learned how to navigate with compasses.

Although China has seen conflict and change throughout its history as control of the country swapped between **dynasties**, scientific knowledge was never lost. Chinese inventors weren't satisfied with 'good-enough' inventions, so they went back to study and perfect the work of past inventors.

The spoon in a Han Dynasty compass was made from a naturally magnetic stone called lodestone. Later, Tang scientists learned to magnetise iron needles by rubbing them with a lodestone.

Gunpowder

MUST BE ABLE TO:

put out fires

Developing new substances through trial and error could be dangerous. Chinese inventors probably burnt their eyebrows (and maybe more!) as early experiments with gunpowder often caused explosions and set buildings on fire! However, by the 10th century, scientists had the formula under control and the Chinese army used gunpowder in flamethrowers and grenades.

EAST MEETS WEST

Between the 8th and 13th centuries, scientists across the **Islamic Empire** revisited ancient ideas to create new scientific theories and develop their own ideas about maths and medicine.

Saving science

Most of the scientific work of the Greeks and Romans was lost in Western Europe after the fall of their empires. However, in the 8th and 9th centuries, Islamic **scholars** in the city of Baghdad (now in modern-day Iraq) managed to track down copies of these texts. Their study and translation of ideas from the past about astronomy, medicine, geography and more saved this ancient knowledge forever.

HAVE YOU GOT WHAT IT TAKES?

TRANSLATOR

MUST HAVE:
A very big dictionary

Islamic scientists had to speak and write multiple languages (and alphabets!) in order to read ancient texts. Most were fluent in Arabic, Greek and **Persian**. These scientists added theories from other civilisations and their own ideas to the translated text to create an ultimate guide to each scientific subject.

Muslim, Christian and Jewish scholars worked together at the House of Wisdom in Baghdad, which had the largest collection of books in the world during the 9th century.

The immense impact of Islamic scientists can be seen in the number of scientific words that begin with 'al', Arabic for 'the', such as algebra, algorithm and alkali. These overachievers also introduced the number system we use today (1, 2, 3 etc), spotted the Andromeda Galaxy, carried out experiments using **control groups** and invented automatic controls for machines. Phew!

This is an Islamic design for an automatic water scoop.

SUPER SCIENTISTS

NAME: Avicenna (c.980–1037)

NATIONALITY: Iranian

AKA: Medical marvel

ACHIEVEMENTS: Avicenna started studying medicine at the age of sixteen and within a few years, had cured a **sultan** of a mysterious illness. Later, he used his mega brain to write at least 240 books about science, based on ancient Greek ideas. One of his books, *The Canon of Medicine*, was used as a medical textbook for over 500 years.

THE RETURN OF SCIENCE

After the end of the Roman Empire, Western Europe was plunged into a time of **illiteracy** and lack of education, known as the **Dark Ages**. It seemed as if many ancient ideas were going to be lost forever.

Greek to Arabic to Latin

In the 12th century, scientific knowledge made an incredible comeback in Europe, thanks to Arabic versions of the long-forgotten ancient texts. However, the new universities that sprung up across Europe in the Middle Ages only taught science that fit in with Christian ideas, such as Ptolemy's model of the universe (see page 9). They didn't encourage their students to make observations or develop new theories.

HAVE YOU GOT WHAT IT TAKES?

ALCHEMIST

PERSONALITY PROFILE:
Mad about metals

Outside of the universities, alchemists were some of the most creative scientists in the Middle Ages. They played around with metals in the hope that they might magically turn into gold or better still, the philosopher's stone, which could make you **immortal**! Alchemy was clearly a load of nonsense, but alchemists did learn a lot about metals from their experiments. Today, this science is known as chemistry.

Little by little, brave scientists dared to question the standard Christian ideas about science and went back to using observation and experiments to explain the world. During the **Renaissance**, educated people started to think about the world in a different way. They valued people-centred subjects, such as history and art, but their inquisitive minds were also intrigued by science.

INGENIOUS INVENTORS

NAME: Leonardo da Vinci (1452–1519)

NATIONALITY: Italian

AKA: Mr Invent-it-all

ACHIEVEMENTS: Although Leonardo trained as an artist, he had an incredible eye for inventions. Many of his designs were forward thinking but impractical, such as his idea for a mechanical robot knight, but some became popular, such as his automatic thread winding machine. Like many other Renaissance men, he also studied a wide range of scientific areas, from fossils and plants to **anatomy** and maths.

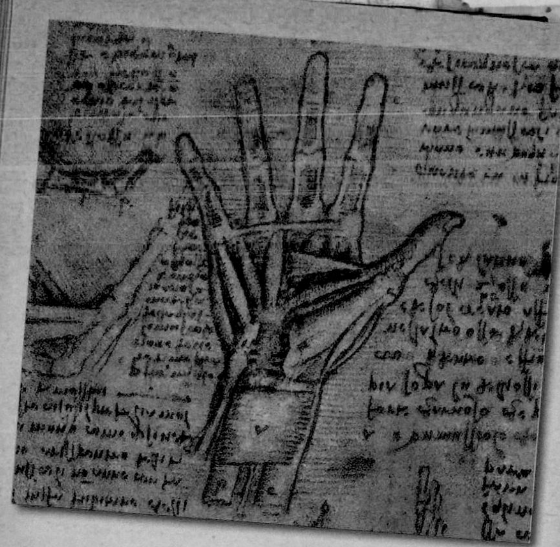

Leonardo dissected dead bodies for art, rather than science! He sketched the bones and muscles and used these details to make his paintings and sculptures more accurate.

Leonardo's famous aerial screw flying machine looks very similar to a modern helicopter. However, scientists have tested Leonardo's design and proved that it doesn't work.

THE SKY'S THE LIMIT

After the printing press finally arrived in Europe in the 15th century, books could be made quickly and cheaply. It had never been easier for scientists to share ideas.

Ideas across Europe

In the early 16th century, the Polish scientist Nicolaus Copernicus came up with the far-out idea that Ptolemy was wrong and that the Sun, not the Earth, was at the centre of the universe. He published his findings in a book, which made its way across Europe to Tycho Brahe in Denmark and Johannes Kepler in Germany. These scientists published books containing revised versions of Copernicus's theory, which were later read by the Italian scientist, Galileo Galilei.

SUPER SCIENTISTS

NAME: Tycho Brahe (1546–1601)

NATIONALITY: Danish

AKA: Secret star spotter

ACHIEVEMENTS: After witnessing a solar eclipse as a teenager, Tycho dedicated his life to studying the stars. He made observations with the **naked eye**, as telescopes had not been invented yet. As a student, he followed Ptolemy's model of the universe, but quickly switched to Copernicus's model after spotting an unknown star in a place where Ptolemy had said no stars could ever be.

In this statue, the model of the universe in Copernicus's hand has a golden ball at its centre to represent the Sun. This model is called the **heliocentric model**.

After reading about the theory of the heliocentric model, Galileo decided to find out the truth. With his homemade telescope, he saw the surface of the Moon and the four moons whizzing around Jupiter. He finally had proof that bodies in space move around objects other than the Earth, which confirmed that the heliocentric model was correct.

Galileo designed and made his own telescope without ever having seen one! He had only heard about telescope and microscope lenses made by glasses makers in the Netherlands.

Galileo drew sketches of the surface of the Moon based on his observations through his telescope.

MUST BE ABLE TO:

apologise publically

The Catholic Church was very unhappy with Galileo's findings, as they went against the idea that the Earth was the centre of everything. They forbid Galileo to teach his ideas and forced him to publically admit that he didn't believe the Sun was at the centre of the universe. He was also sentenced to life imprisonment in his luxurious house – harder to complain about that one!

...ILAEI INVENTVM.ET OPVS,QVO SOLIS MACVLAS,
...ES, ET IOVIS SATELLITES,ET NOVAM QVASI
...ITATE PRIMVS DISPEXIT A.MDCIX.

PROVING A POINT

In the 17th and 18th centuries, scientific societies (clubs) were all the rage with rich, educated men. They got together to chat about science, perform exciting experiments and publish their findings.

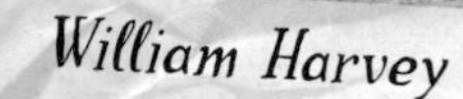
William Harvey

The English scientist William Harvey dissected animals to show this crowd of scientists how the heart pumps blood around the body.

HAVE YOU GOT WHAT IT TAKES?

GUINEA PIG

MUST HAVE: Trust in yourself

It was often easier for scientists to try out their crazy experiments on themselves, rather than convince other people to take part. One Italian scientist spent 30 years weighing everything that went into (and out of) his body as part of an experiment. In the 19th century, one doctor rubbed his body with the vomit of a **yellow fever** patient to prove that the disease wasn't contagious. Yuck!

Prove it!

Most society members followed the scientific method, an idea that dates back to Aristotle (see page 7). They believed that scientists needed to prove their ideas to be true by testing, observation, or carrying out experiments in front of all the society members. The Royal Society in London was so keen on the scientific method that their motto was *Nullius in verba* – 'Take nobodys word for it' in Latin!

With so many brilliant minds together in one society, jealousy was only natural. Feedback from other Royal Society members helped scientists to improve and perfect theories, but sometimes it was hard to hear the truth. Competitive friendships quickly turned into bitter rivalries.

A meeting of the Royal Society in London. Isaac Newton is sitting in the chair at the back.

MUST BE ABLE TO:

deal with criticism

The top Royal Society frenemies were Isaac Newton, a physicist and mathematician, and Robert Hooke, a scientist who demonstrated experiments for the other members. It all kicked off when Hooke badmouthed Newton's reflecting telescope, which used mirrors rather than the lenses used in Galileo's telescope, even though Newton's telescope worked really well. Newton was so angry with Hooke that he stopped going to Royal Society meetings for a while!

HE SAID WHAT?

'To explain all nature is too difficult a task for any one man or even for any one age.'

Isaac Newton

STEAMING AHEAD

The inventions of the **Industrial Revolution** in 18th century Britain changed our world forever. People no longer needed to make objects by hand – machines could do it for them!

Super steam

The **steam engine**, a machine that uses steam to power machines, was the top invention of the Industrial Revolution. This handy machine was used at every stage of the process of creating objects – to power the machines that collected raw materials, to run factory machines and in ships and trains to transport goods.

MUST BE ABLE TO:
work with others

It took several people quite a while to get the steam engine working exactly right! Two early inventors went into business together after finding out that they would have to share a **patent** as their designs were so similar. The Scottish inventor, James Watt, perfected the steam engine with the help of cash and tips from other inventors.

The well-preserved steam-powered looms in Quarry Bank Mill, Cheshire, are still used to weave cloth today! In previous centuries, cloth was woven on hand-powered looms.

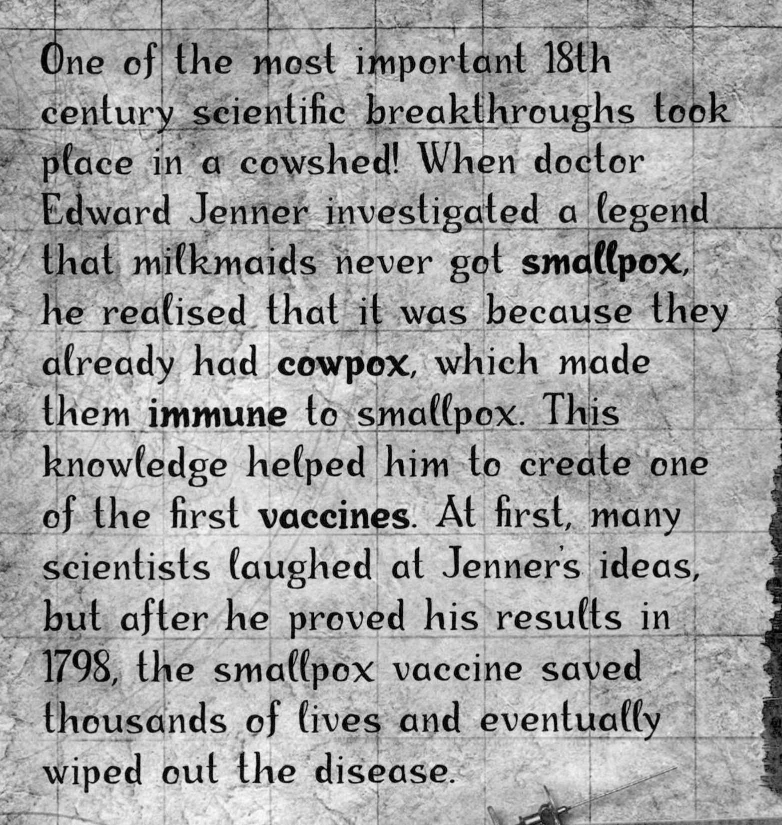

One of the most important 18th century scientific breakthroughs took place in a cowshed! When doctor Edward Jenner investigated a legend that milkmaids never got **smallpox**, he realised that it was because they already had **cowpox**, which made them **immune** to smallpox. This knowledge helped him to create one of the first **vaccines**. At first, many scientists laughed at Jenner's ideas, but after he proved his results in 1798, the smallpox vaccine saved thousands of lives and eventually wiped out the disease.

MUST BE ABLE TO:

get your hands dirty

To get the ingredients for his vaccine, Jenner had to collect pus from a cowpox blister! However, this was nothing compared to Louis Pasteur, a later developer of vaccines. He had to collect spit from the mouth of a dangerous **rabid** dog to use in his rabies vaccine!

SCIENCE GOES BOOM!

After the Industrial Revolution, it was much easier for 19th century scientists and inventors to travel and get their hands on materials for their experiments. This led to an explosion of new and exciting ideas.

Shocking stuff

Many 19th century inventions, such as the **telegraph** and the telephone, were powered by one of the century's most electrifying developments – the electrical current. These inventions were so popular with everyday people that inventors went into overdrive, searching for the next big hit.

HAVE YOU GOT WHAT IT TAKES?

TEAM LEADER

TOP SKILL: Patenting what's popular

Thomas Edison realised that popular inventions could lead to big bucks, so he set up a team to develop new inventions for him to patent. In total, Edison patented a whopping 1,093 inventions, including the light bulb and the motion picture camera. However, Edison wasn't always the best boss. He lost one of his star inventors, Nikola Tesla, after a big fight. Tesla went solo and developed the electricity system used to power buildings today.

This is a recreation of the research lab where Edison's team worked.

Before the 19th century, only a few rich men had access to a good scientific education. This changed in the 19th century, when European governments set up technical schools to teach science to a larger audience. Poor but brainy scientists could also win money through awards, which helped them pay for materials.

Finch specimens collected by Darwin in the Galápagos Islands.

HAVE YOU GOT WHAT IT TAKES?

**** EXPLORER ****

MUST HAVE: A taste for travel

With advances in shipbuilding, and the invention of the steam engine, around-the-world travel became faster and more affordable. Scientists could travel the globe in search of exotic animals and plants to research. The specimens that Charles Darwin found on his five-year-long trip on the HMS *Beagle* inspired his theory of **evolution by natural selection.**

SUPER SCIENTISTS

NAME: Ada Lovelace (1815–1852)

NATIONALITY: English

KNOWN FOR: Analytical aptitude

ACHIEVEMENTS: Not all 19th century scientists were able to study science. Ada Lovelace didn't go to school because she was a girl, so top scientists and mathematicians taught her at home. She was fascinated by Charles Babbage's Analytical Engine (AE) – a type of early computer. Even though the AE was never actually built, Ada figured how to make this imaginary machine calculate a sequence of numbers, making her the world's first computer programmer.

UP AND AWAY

After the boom of inventions in the 19th century, science made huge strides in the early 20th century. Some scientists even worried that they would discover all of the science in the world within a few decades!

More and more

However, these scientists had nothing to worry about. Top scientists such as Albert Einstein and the Curies continued to make groundbreaking discoveries, about **relativity** and **radioactivity**. The Curies' research into X-rays allows us to safely use this life-saving equipment today.

Marie Curie and her husband Pierre worked together to research radioactivity. On her own, Marie discovered two new **elements**.

MUST BE ABLE TO:

avoid radiation poisoning

Although early X-rays often caused burns and hair loss, no one knew quite how dangerous **radiation** was in the early 20th century. While researching radiation, Marie Curie often felt sick and tired, with raw swollen hands, but that didn't put her off her work. Sadly, she died at the age of 66 of a disease caused by radiation. Today, scientists keep radioactive elements in protective cases and wear special suits.

SHE SAID WHAT?

'Nothing in life is to be feared, it is only to be understood.'

Marie Curie

Humans have always dreamed of being able to fly but it wasn't until the early 20th century that we finally got off the ground in the first aeroplanes, designed by the Wright brothers. Not all 20th century inventions were as spectacular as flying machines, but for those that could afford them, domestic appliances such as vacuum cleaners and televisions made life easier and more fun.

HAVE YOU GOT WHAT IT TAKES?

*** SHOWMAN ***

TOP SKILL: Putting on a performance

After the Wright brothers made their first successful plane flight in 1903, they were disappointed that no one believed they had done it! To prove their critics wrong, they gave public demonstrations of their planes and free rides to important people. It wasn't long before planes caught on in a big way.

The first televisions in the 1920s and '30s were very expensive.

All those knobs but only one channel!

Vacuum tube

OUT OF THIS WORLD

As the 20th century went on, our understanding of science skyrocketed. For the first time, humans travelled into space and learned more about the science beyond Earth.

The Hubble Space Telescope has made over 1.2 million observations since its launch, including stunning images of nebulae (clouds of dust in space).

Racing into space

After sending humans into space for short missions, such as the *Apollo 11* Moon landing of 1969, scientists looked for ways to observe space over longer periods of time. The Hubble Space Telescope has orbited the Earth since 1990, taking photos of stars and galaxies up to 13.4 billion light years away. Back on Earth, scientists such as Stephen Hawking formed theories about the formation of the universe.

HE SAID WHAT?

'My goal is simple. It is a complete understanding of the universe, why it is as it is and why it exists at all.'

Stephen Hawking

SUPER SCIENTISTS

NAME: Stephen Hawking (1942–)

NATIONALITY: English

KNOWN FOR: Bigging up the **Big Bang**

ACHIEVEMENTS: After his work on mysterious black holes helped to prove that the Big Bang created the universe, Hawking wanted to share his ideas with everyone. He became famous for writing books that explain complicated scientific ideas in a language that everyone could understand.

During the 20th century, inventors transformed computers from large, clunky machines used for research to pocket-sized, everyday items found in almost every home. Computer programming allows us to play games, store information and interpret data with the click of a button. People on opposite sides of the world can work together and share new ideas, thanks to the Internet.

Margaret Hamilton with the code that she wrote for the on-board computer in the *Apollo 11* spacecraft, used in the first Moon landing in 1969.

INGENIOUS INVENTORS

NAME: Tim Berners-Lee (1955–)

NATIONALITY: English

AKA: World Wide Web whiz

ACHIEVEMENTS: In the 1970s, scientists developed the Internet as a way of connecting computers together so that they could email each other directly. In 1989, Tim Berners-Lee got sick of emailing and he came up with a way of posting documents on the Internet so that other people could see them. Today, this system is called the World Wide Web and the documents are known as websites.

TOMMOROW'S WORLD

Thanks to the Internet, ordinary people are more aware of scientific discoveries and inventions than ever before. Children learn about science and technology at school, sparking an interest that could lead to the next big breakthrough.

Can we, should we?

Today, people across the world debate the **ethics** of scientific experiments that push the bounds of science, such as **genetic engineering**. After discovering and thoroughly researching **DNA** in the 20th century, scientists now know enough about genes to be able to change them. Although genetic engineering could help to stop some diseases, many people question what the consequences of changing the makeup of living things would be.

Some scientists want to use genetic engineering to bring back extinct animals, such as woolly mammoths. Watch out for the tusks!

MUST BE ABLE TO:

speak English

As collaboration between scientists from different countries is so common nowadays, the language of science is usually English. Having one language in common makes it easier for international scientists to work together in laboratories and read research from all across the world.

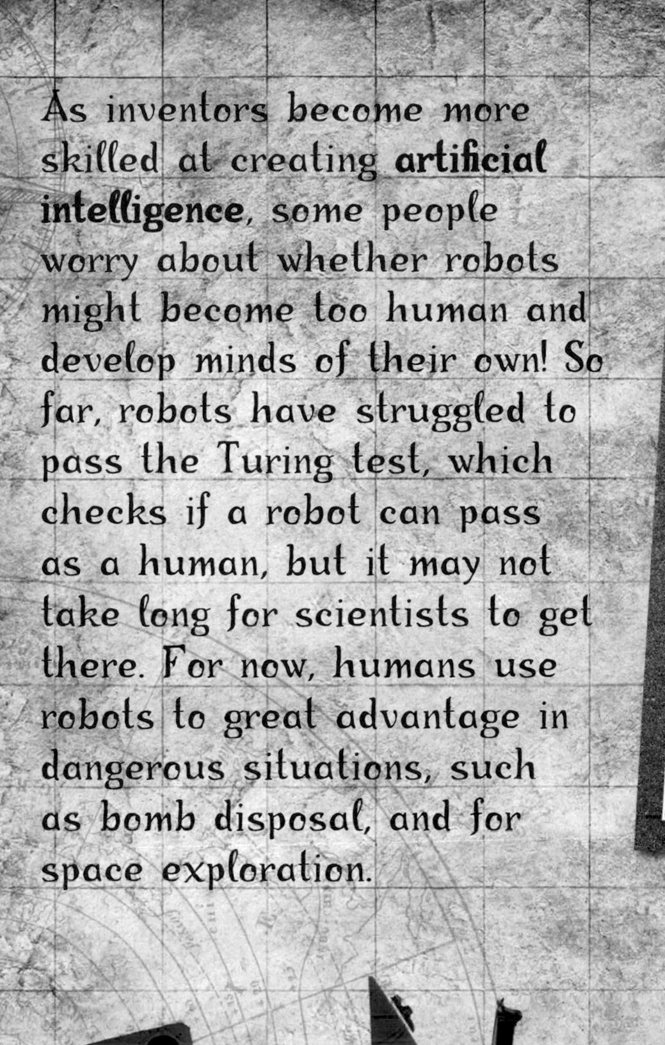

As inventors become more skilled at creating **artificial intelligence**, some people worry about whether robots might become too human and develop minds of their own! So far, robots have struggled to pass the Turing test, which checks if a robot can pass as a human, but it may not take long for scientists to get there. For now, humans use robots to great advantage in dangerous situations, such as bomb disposal, and for space exploration.

HAVE YOU GOT WHAT IT TAKES?

VIRTUAL VIRTUOSO

TOP SKILL: Website insight

Most modern inventors no longer work with bubbling test tubes and clockwork parts, or even create objects that you can hold in your hands, but their virtual applications and programmes have revolutionised our lives. Today, over 1.59 billion people around the world use the website Facebook, created by Mark Zuckerberg, to chat, share photos and watch videos.

HE SAID WHAT?

'The biggest risk is not taking any risk. In a world that's changing really quickly, the only strategy that is guaranteed to fail is not taking risks.'

Mark Zuckerberg

Humans have not yet been able to travel to Mars, but we have learned a lot about the planet from the data collected by the Mars Curiosity Rover.

GLOSSARY

anatomy – the study of the human body and how its parts are arranged

aqueduct – a structure for carrying water across land

artificial intelligence – the study and development of computer systems that do jobs that normally require human intelligence

BCE – the letters BCE stand for 'before common era'. They refer to dates up until the year CE 1.

Big Bang – the explosion of matter across the universe that many scientists believe to be the beginning of our universe

bile – a liquid in our bodies that breaks down fat

CE – the letters CE stand for 'common era'. They refer to dates after the year CE 1.

control group – a group of people who are used for comparison in an experiment

cowpox – a disease similar to smallpox that causes spots on the body

Dark Ages – the period in western Europe between the fall of the Roman Empire and the Middle Ages

dissect – to cut something into pieces for scientific study

DNA – a chemical in cells that contains genetic information

dynasty – a series of rulers who are all from the same family

element – one of more than one hundred different substances on Earth. Everything on Earth is made from one or more different elements.

empire – a group of countries under the control of one country

ethics – ideas about whether something is right or wrong

evolution by natural selection – the way in which living things change over time to become more suited to their surroundings

genetic engineering – the activity of changing the genes of a plant or an animal

geocentric model – a model of the universe that places the Earth at its centre

heliocentric model – a model of the universe that places the Sun at its centre

illiteracy – not being able to read or write

immortal – describes something or someone that lives forever

immune – if you are immune to a disease, you will not catch it

Industrial Revolution – a period of time in which the development of machines led to huge changes in society. In Britain, the Industrial Revolution happened in the 18th century.

logic – a way of thinking that is based on reason rather than emotions

Middle Ages – a period of time between the 12th and 15th centuries

naked eye – if something can be seen with the naked eye, it is big enough to be seen without special equipment

orbit – to follow a curved path around a planet or star

papyrus – a type of grass that can be made into a paper-like sheet

patent – a licence that a company or person receives for their product so that no one else can copy it

Persian – a language spoken in Iran

philosopher – someone who studies the meaning of life

phlegm – a liquid made in your lungs, throat and nose when you have a cold

physician – a doctor

rabid – describes someone or something that is suffering from rabies, a serious disease

radiation – energy that comes from a nuclear reaction, which can hurt you

radioactivity – how much radiation something gives out

relativity – the relationship between time and objects in space

Renaissance – a period between the 14th and 16th centuries in Europe when there was a lot of interest in art and literature

scholar – someone who has studied a subject and knows a lot about it

Silk Road – a trade route linking China with the Middle East

smallpox – a disease that causes a fever and spots on the body

steam engine – a machine part that uses energy from steam to create power

sultan – a ruler of a part of the Islamic Empire

supernatural – something that can't be explained by science

taboo – something that is not said or done because people think it is morally wrong

telegraph – an old-fashioned system of sending messages using radio or electrical signals

theory – an idea that is used to explain something

vaccine – a substance that is given to people to stop them catching a disease

yellow fever – a disease that makes the skin turn yellow

STATES AND EMPIRES

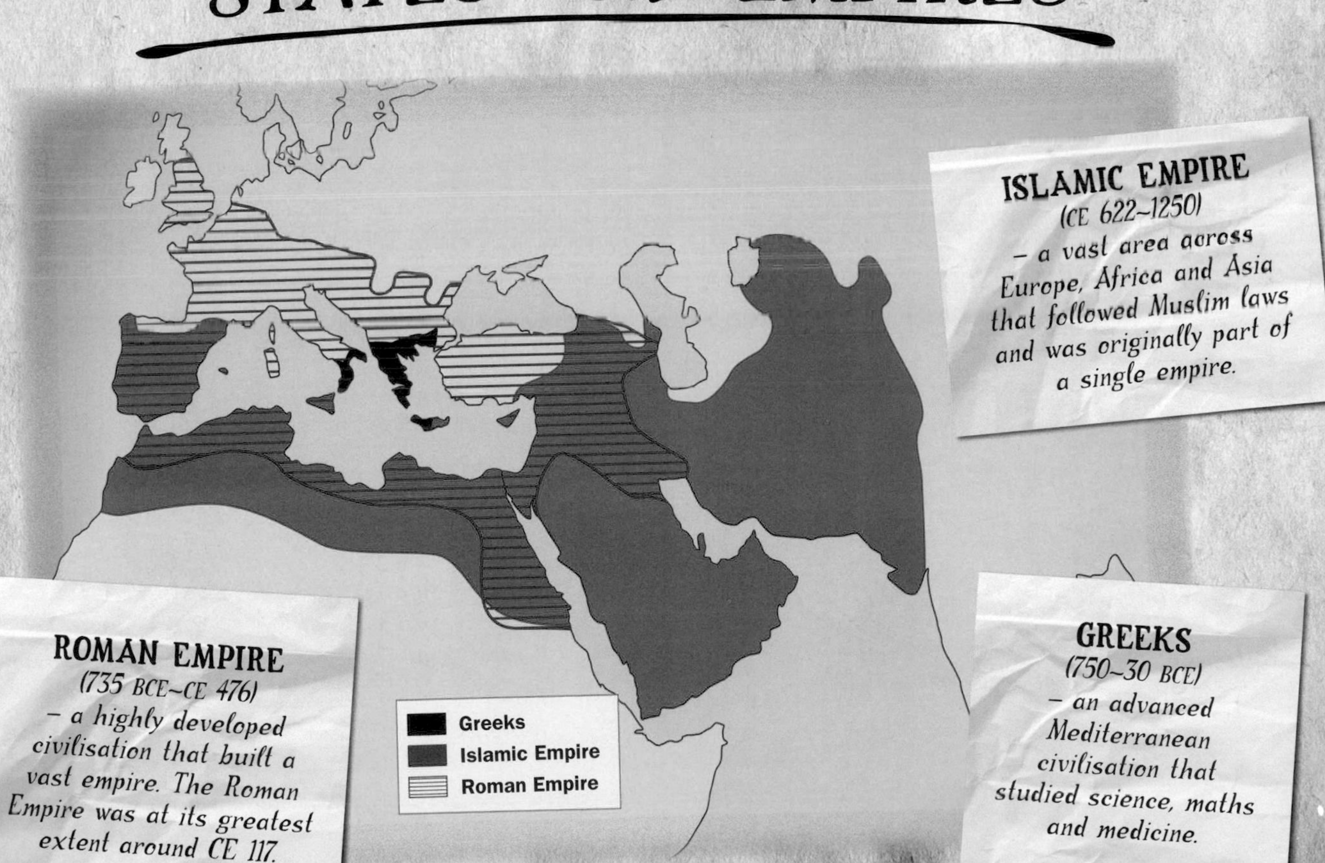

ISLAMIC EMPIRE
(CE 622–1250)
– a vast area across Europe, Africa and Asia that followed Muslim laws and was originally part of a single empire.

ROMAN EMPIRE
(735 BCE–CE 476)
– a highly developed civilisation that built a vast empire. The Roman Empire was at its greatest extent around CE 117.

GREEKS
(750–30 BCE)
– an advanced Mediterranean civilisation that studied science, maths and medicine.

INDEX

Further information

http://www.dkfindout.com/uk/science/amazing-inventions/

Learn more about great inventions and their inventors.

https://www.esa.int/esaKIDSen/SEMLWAXJD1E_OurUniverse_0.html

Enjoy an animated history of astronomy and space exploration.

http://knowitall.org/kidswork/hospital/history/ancient/index.html

Explore a timeline of changes and developments in medicine.

3 0116 02035232 2